Get The Click

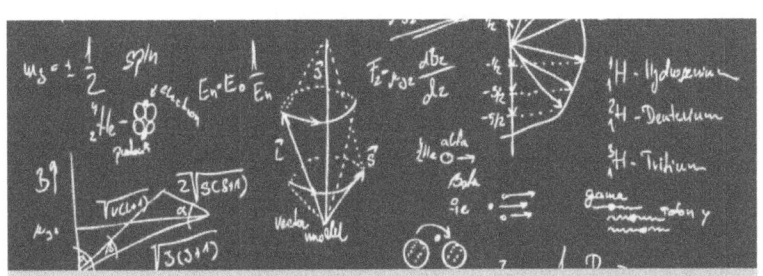

Legal Disclaimer

Table of Contents

Get The Click 1

.... 1

Legal Disclaimer 2

Table of Contents... 3

Chapter 1 Why You Need "Get The Click" 4

Chapter 2 How to Create Your Perfect Customer (From the Start!) 14

Chapter 3 How to Create Your Perfect Customer Avatar in 3 Steps 17

Chapter 4 Create Your USP in 17 Minutes!.. 20

Chapter 5 The Perfect USP... 23

Chapter 6 Combining AIDA with PAS For Multiplied Response................................. 24

Chapter 7 The Secret Recipe.. 25

About The Author 37

More from Doug Barger... 39

One Last Thing... 40

Chapter 1 Why You Need "Get The Click"

Could you use more quality (cash-spending buyers) traffic to your website?

If you want to prosper with your online business you most definitely can.

What a huge problem it is most people experience online when it comes to getting traffic.

The problem is they are doing a lot of work without seeing the kind of results they could be

enjoying easily by just making a few simple adjustments.

So you want to get the most out of your every effort right?

(No one wants to spend unneeded time and energy for less results than they deserve.)

And with these easy to implement strategies to get more bang for your buck and traffic to your

website with your marketing, you're about to discover simple formulas professional marketing

experts have relied on for years...

...to maximize results quickly with every marketing material, promotional piece, every article

they publish, every sales letter they write and even scripts on videos they create.

You will also see a new improvement that enhances the old model by taking the best components of two of the most effective formulas and combining them into one new super direct response formula that is the foundation of the winning "Get The Click" formula.

When it really comes down to it, you could substitute the word "click" with these words:

- action
- sale
- subscription
- response

   It only depends on the specific medium you use and the action you want your prospect, lead, customer or client to take.

The reason these secret weapons work so well for you, is because they appeal to basic human nature and consumer behavioral psychology when it comes to marketing.

Okay, the order really is important because of the way we process information so pay particular attention to the order of each of these mechanisms when the time comes later to learn the formula so you can implement it most effectively and enjoy the best success.

But before we dive straight into the meat of the formula, I believe it's important to start with the "why" of the formula so you know exactly what you're getting with this formula and have a solid understanding of the best ways you can apply it right away to everything you do.
Once you have completed reading, understanding and learning the entire formula, you will undoubtedly experience a "light bulb" effect where you will see everything you've done in business and marketing up to this point in a whole new light and best of all, be ready to take your business to a whole new level of results, profits and growth.

So *why* is it so important for you to learn to use the

Get The Click Formula?

Quite simply, because of all the benefits you get using the formula that you just can't get without it.

What are these benefits you can expect to enjoy once you use the "Get The Click" formula?

Not to sound cryptic, but surprisingly many more than meet the eye.

For starters, when you get more clicks, from more qualified prospects, who click on your free content, you can offer them a product for free that you use to provide them value and generate free leads for your business.

Let's look at one of the most popular and profitable online business models before we get into how you will use the formula, so that you will have a frame of reference to help you picture how your marketing content optimized with the Get The Click formula can effectively increase your overall traffic, quality of that traffic, lead flow, customers, repeat customers, referrals and every part of your business that depends on someone taking an action.

One of the most popular business models online is the tried and proven business model where you in essence set up your marketing system that leads with an introductory offer as a loss leader. Your visitor reads your strategically placed content and clicks on your link after being directed by your strategically placed call to action. By the time your prospect reaches the call to action, you have already used the qualifying component of the Get The Click Formula to ensure it is a qualified prospect who clicks on your link.

So that is only one of the many important advantages of using the Get The Click formula to power the marketing of your business. You instantly generate more *qualified* leads and sales to customers who are prescreened automatically to be perfect for your offer before they ever go online to search for it and find it.

Perhaps <u>nothing is more important in marketing than "message to market match"</u>.

This simply means your message to your market is one that resonates with your prospects in a way where they can tell you are intimately acquainted with the most important issues they deal with on a daily basis and you are qualified to solve their problems by virtue of this with your products and services supplying the solutions they want and need.

In the big picture this means you "get" your market and you "click" with them. This is far more important than any individual click on a link (although you'll soon see it's also the most important component to generating that result). You "Get The Click".

It's much like when you turn the dial on a combination lock and you have everything lined up just right, you unlock it and it becomes open and accessible to you.

So your marketing is the secret combination that opens the market's wallet to you.

When they click on your link, they are redirected to a landing page where you offer a product that solves the problem most people in their niche market struggle with the most. In order to access the product for free, they simply agree to subscribe to your mailing list by typing their name and best email in the web form on your website.

The web form is created by a programming code that takes their details and instantly stores it in a back office database for you where you collect leads.

I know a lot of people use marketing mumbo-jumbo and jargon, but that's not my style. So just in case you're unsure what is meant by "web form", here is a picture of what one looks like. It is one I use on one of my fan pages at Facebook.

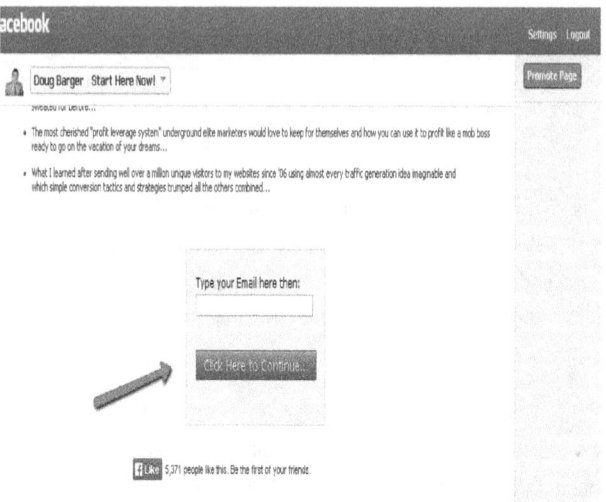

This is a web form where subscribers can join one of my lists.

Pay particular attention to the "action" button on the web form illustrated above with the words "Click Here to Continue…

You can see instead of using the word "submit" like many web forms do, this call to action is:

1. Clear
2. *Specific*
3. Direct

Why is this important?

The reason this is so important is because this is an *extremely important* part of your sales process and if you get this part wrong it can destroy your response rate.

So many people get this wrong it isn't funny. They are literally throwing their time and advertising dollars away when they could turn this "front door" into their business into a profit generating powerhouse with only a few simple tweaks.

I don't care what kind of analytics you're using to measure your response rate, but you need to use something.

For many years, I used the free tool available from Google called "Google Analytics".

Not only is it free, but it's simple to install the tracking code and helps you track all the behavior of the visitors to your website so you know what's working and what's not.

This database of leads is called your "mailing list" or "e-mail list", "subscriber list", "customer list" or just "list".

The beauty of growing your list of subscribers this way is you can use an autoresponder service to send your entire list of subscribers a message via e-mail simultaneously with just one click of the "send" broadcast button located within the admin panel dashboard of your autoresponder list management software account.

You can also preload your autoresponder with messages sequentially in your list management software's back office and set the date and time for your subscribers to get the email.

If your tracking of opens and clicks begin to show you trends like most of your customers open and click their e-mails they get from you when you send them at 8:00am eastern or 9:00am central time zone, then you can begin to send your messages during that time instead of later to get more response. This is just one simple way of using metrics to adjust your e-mail marketing so you can optimize it for measurable quantifiable improvements.

For another example, you can set a series of 20 messages to go out automatically to each new subscriber starting the day they subscribe where they each get a new message every two days with a day apart scheduled in between to space out the frequency.

This means, they'd get a message from you every other day for forty days in a row.

Here is what it looks like inside the online back office of your autoresponder list management software account where you manage your list as well as automated messages you preload to your software and schedule to send in advance, as well as live broadcasts when you have news or a more timely announcement to make.

You can create unlimited follow up messages to send as a series and schedule when to send them and how many days apart.

Industry statistics for the last ten years have suggested it normally takes anywhere from 5 to 7 contacts via e-mail before a subscriber who subscribed for free will make a purchase from a link inside an email you send them. There could be many reasons for this, but the general consensus is one I happen to agree with simply because it just makes sense and the numbers support it. If you've studied business and especially sales as it applies to business and marketing your business, you've likely heard the maxim, "People buy from who they know, like and trust."

When you have a process set up to build a relationship of communication based on addressing a need your prospect has and then follow that up with a solution to give them what they want to solve their problem, you have done the necessary work to be perceived by your prospect as someone they know, like and trust enough to buy products from you.

Now, back to this link inside your email: It should be a link to your product you offer them at a "low ticket" compared with your other higher end products and services to where it doesn't cost much for them to try out your products. Remember, you used the free item to overcome the hurdle of trust building the first time. This is how and why they are on your list in the first place.

Provided that you supplied a good value for them with a product that lived up to the promise of solving the problem they had, then you will have already positioned yourself as someone who they can trust to buy from due to the trust you've built with that first product.

This first paid product you offer them will fulfill a similar purpose, except that instead of asking for them to type their name and email and agree to get marketing messages from you in exchange for the product, you are asking them to click on the order link and make a small purchase from you to get a product that provides even more value than the original free one and that solves either another problem they face or offers them more ways to reach a common goal most people in that niche face.

Ideally, you can even use a free survey creation software to poll your list of subscribers and ask them to tell you what problems are most important to them to solve, what solutions they are most looking to buy and you could even ask them to name what content a product you offer them must contain before they would buy it from you and then use that information to build a product based on established demand.

I can guarantee you one thing, if you ask your prospects and customers what they need and want to buy from you and then create your products based on what they told you, you will have really done more for your business than you can imagine and will have built up more trust that should lead to more purchases of higher ticket items from you.

This is the power of using the Get The Click cash creation response formula to transform quality qualified prospects into leads and then transform those leads into customers who go on to be your best clients who purchase high ticket products and services from you regularly.

The best part is, every content you create whether it be ad copy to sell a product, an article to presell your prospects on your product, a blog post you can use to presell, an email, a video script…you are unlimited in that you can use the formula with any media you choose and will want to apply "Get The Click" to all the content you currently use and every piece of content you create in the future.

Master this one formula and you can grow your business both fast and predictably profitably.

Chapter 2 How to Create Your Perfect Customer (From the Start!)

It's one thing to know some basic information about characteristics most of your customers share, like demographics that include: ages, locations, highest level of education completed, household income, marital status, number of kids and… the list can continue with as much data as you like.

It's quite another thing altogether when you can determine who your ideal customer is *before* you do business and gear all your marketing efforts based on what you know about them.

This one simple shift in approach can radically increase the quality, success and as a by-product, the profitability of your business many and many times over again.

I want you to think about exactly why this approach is more effective at producing better results for you when you use it instead of any other way and I will help you "get it".

Let's oversimplify the concept with an example that makes it easier to "get". When I was first learning business and marketing, I used to always hear experts and coaches preach the importance of knowing your target prospect.

The only problem was, I didn't know how it was possible to know who they were *before* they bought something. I mean, we were supposed to be some kind of prophet who sees the future or spy on people to see all their buying habits and then pounce on them?

If it was the latter, then I definitely wasn't interested because all that kind of stuff felt slimy to me. You know what I mean? For some reason, that was one of the areas where I had a tough time really understanding how it worked as a concept until I got to see it in action and see the difference it made.

But once I got it, it really clicked in a big way -- and I believe it will for you too.

So here's what this idea is all about. Let's say you have a group of Antarctic natives who decide they will never leave Antarctica as one potential group and then on the other end of the spectrum, you have a group of college students who are going from a northern state in the United States down to the sunny state of Florida for spring break vacation.

So one group in ice and snow with igloos and the other in sunshine and beach time fun. Not absolutely and completely polar opposites, but pretty close to being opposite when it comes to climate.

Now obviously this is an extremely different group of people just going by how one is hot and the other cold, but the more "different" I could make them, the better I feel it helps you to really "get" the idea so you'll be able to apply it when the differences aren't so dramatic.

You still with me, so far?

Okay good. So we start with super easy and then graduate to almost imperceptible subtle differences that give you the advantage in ways your competition doesn't even realize exist. So back to this super easy example and just bear with me a bit here now because you'll want to thank me for it later and just trust me until you see it, okay?

Okay, so you wouldn't spend your advertising and marketing budgets on ads and marketing materials created for the Florida spring break vacation people and try to sell them igloo related products to help them with their igloos would you?

Of course not. So you know from the start, with this oversimplified example, you would be focusing your efforts, time and budget (money) on reaching the best possible candidate for your product, the one who needs it the most and has the most to gain from it.

Why? Simple. You want to stretch each dollar of your budget as far as it will go and get the most bang for your marketing buck and advertising dollar as you possibly can.

The more you do it that way, the more profitable of a business you have and the more you can focus precious time, energy and resources like money on better serving your best customers because they are the ones who are the backbone of your business.

So, with this example, we see the closer aligned your advertising and marketing efforts are geared toward your most ideal customer, the more money you make and the less money you lose. We can see why it makes all the sense (and dollars) in the world to make sure you know exactly who is your best customer before you begin to reach them.

So is it really possible to start with those Antarctic igloo owners (instead of the college kids going to spring break vacation) and only sell to them and be successful with your campaign without chasing after unqualified prospects who would only waste your time because they weren't the ideal prospects for your offer from the very start?

The answer is yes.

So how do you actually go about doing this?

This is where you learn to <u>create your perfect customer avatar</u>. In fact, you'll get the 3 step method for creating an avatar for up to 4 different segments of your niche market.

You've probably heard at least a dozen (if not more) business and marketing experts talk about creating your customer avatar, but chances are, they kind of hurried through that part if your experience was much like mine.

You would think something like, "That's really great that you know how to do that, but how am I supposed to benefit from it, if it's so important like you say it is, but you never actually come out and show me how to do it?"

Talk about frustrating. And yes, I felt your pain and still do just remembering it.

That's why I felt it was important enough to give you a guide with examples and walk you through the steps of creating your own avatar for your perfect customer.

Now pay close attention. If you will really try to understand this on the following pages, until you're sure you "get it", then you will be able to improve your business and marketing results dramatically.

It's not just the "understanding" of it that makes the difference, but the actual doing it that will make the difference for you. If you get this down, this guide has paid for itself many times over for years to come already. ☺

Are you ready?

Great!

Let's go…

Chapter 3 How to Create Your Perfect Customer Avatar in 3 Steps

Developing your customer avatar is one of the best things you can do to increase your business marketability and profitability. A customer avatar is simply a means by which you create a model of your best customer. Your best customer is most likely a person who will come to you to purchase products or services over and over again. You will create an avatar based on this.

Here are the 3 basic steps which will help you to develop your customer avatar;

Step 1

Look for at least 10 most popular hangouts

The first step you need to take is to research on the customer demographics and psychographics. This will not be possible unless you find out where these people like to hangout. Ask yourself questions such as the keyword phrases they use on Google, what they are likely to look for and how your product or service will provide a solution. After that, you need to calculate the average number of the age groups available, genders, their interests and other related issues such as where they are likely to work and live. Using tools such as Quantcast.com may help you to find out who your audience should be, whether married or not, the average number of kids they should have and their lifestyle based on their likely income.

By knowing the age group and all the possible information about the lives of your customer avatar, you will be in a position to create your avatar.

Here is an example;

"I will call my avatar Andy. Andy is a 26 year old single mother of 3, who earns an average salary of $25,000. She likes to spend her free time shopping with friends, swimming with her kids and also meeting new people on the famous social site; Facebook. Her husband passed away a few years back leaving her to take care of the three kids on her own. Paying the bills is what she struggles with everyday as she has no help and has to depend on her salary of $25,000. This makes her look for another source of income online. After this she can finally make an extra $2000 a month."

Remember to create emotional triggers throughout your avatar story.

Step 2

Use sites like Facebook to find "likes" for your business

This social site is being used by most people regardless of their age. It will come in handy as you can post different products and services and wait to see what your chosen audience will show interest in. It is also a good way of advertising.

Step 3

Put yourself in the shoes of your target audience.

You ought to know what they will think or feel about your product. It is also up to you to know the possible things they will be told by friends about what your business is offering.

Do you think they will gain from your business?

If so, what are the possible fears being experienced which would make them opt for your competition?

By having ready answers to such questions, you will have enough information to help you create around four avatars for you to use.

When choosing your avatars, you should create at least one for all the age groups you came up with. This will help you increase your earnings as a result of better marketing techniques for all the reasons we already covered.

Before you continue, you may want to go ahead and get out a sheet of paper with a pen to start making a list of the information about your target customer using the guidelines and steps we already covered in this chapter.

The reason it is important to have this already in place before the next chapter is because the next chapter involves creating your unique selling proposition. You will take the list you make now when creating your customer avatar and then use it with the steps provided in the next chapter to create a strong USP.

Once you have your avatar in place, it should only take you no more than about 17 minutes to flesh out a working USP. Eventually you'll whittle it down to its most concise and tested form, but to actually create one that is good enough to start using will only take you a few minutes if you'll just follow the directions of creating your customer avatar and then go through the steps of the process to create your USP in the next chapter.

And when you have both your customer avatar and USP completed, you will own something very powerful from which you can use as the foundation to create all your advertising and marketing materials from this point now and carry it with you into your more successful future.

So that's something to get pretty excited about. When you think about it, it really makes perfect sense too. When you have codified the specifics of your own customer avatar combined with a winning unique selling proposition, you will not only have a picture of who your perfect customer is and know what they want to buy, you'll be able to speak to them in language that speaks to their core desires and core fears. You'll have such a message to market match that combining this knowledge with the formulas you're about to learn in the Get the Click selling formulas part of the system, you'll be armed to the teeth with so many more weapons of raw selling power than your competitors, they won't know why suddenly so many people that would usually buy from them are now flocking to buy from you instead.

But *you* will.

Chapter 4 Create Your USP in 17 Minutes!

A unique selling proposition is the essence of the marketing strategies of all successful businesses. Without a unique selling proposition, your marketing efforts may turn out to be futile. There is a fact that is often ignored by most businesses, which is this:

"...Every prospective customer already has a favorite brand which they are loyal to. Therefore, the goal of every new business is to snatch customers from their competitors. The market is already there, people are already buying. You just have to give them a plausible reason to switch to your brand..."

It's that simple and even more if you are capable of creating an effective unique selling proposition – something you can do in just seventeen minutes if you just read then follow the steps below, but only after you have created your customer avatar from earlier first. With these two crucial elements combined, you will be unstoppable.

Follow the steps below to achieve this.

How to Develop an Effective Unique Selling Proposition (USP)

1. Know your ideal customer: Obviously, you need a pen and a piece of paper for this exercise. Your ideal customer is one that seeks the products or services you concentrate on mainly. For example, you might have a business that involves selling kid shoes as its primary function, but you may also sell toys at the same time in case anyone needs them alongside the shoes they bought.

Now, your ideal customer is not a parent looking for shoes and toys, but shoes only - and you don't have to stop there; you have to go deeper, e.g. a parent looking for high quality but affordable kid shoes for Christmas. The more specific your business is, i.e. tailored to a particular audience, the easier it will be to create a highly effective and compelling USP.

2. Identify the problems your business can resolve: Can your business solve your prospective customers' problems and make their lives easier? If yes, what exactly are those problems? Using the same example above, let's assume there are many families looking for high quality Christmas shoes at affordable prices but no store seems to offer the shoes at reasonable prices.

You could go into that market and fill that gap. Your USP will be more attractive to potential customers if you are addressing a need that no other company is addressing.

Using a very popular and successful USP from several years ago as an example, Domino's Pizza, in their USP, assert that they will deliver your pizza within 30 minutes. They are addressing a need (fast pizza when hunger strikes and you can't cook) that other companies didn't seem to pay attention to. So this example uses the need for speed. It skyrocketed Domino's market share in the pizza industry even when most experts didn't think they'd have a chance against all the giants in the industry at the time. This shows you the power to really take over market share when you create a strong USP and market it aggressively.

So the key with that one was not only were they promising a great benefit, but they were promising a great benefit their top competitors had failed to offer.

If they didn't research their market and create their customer avatar, they might have never even realized that speed of product/service delivery was a customer desire that was going unmet.

Incidentally, Domino's has since changed their USP after one of their drivers was rushing to deliver one within the 30 minute deadline and ran over an old lady.

But we still take away the very valuable example of what a strong USP is, what a strong USP does and the "hows and whys" of doing it.

3. Include the top advantages of your business to customers: Ever heard of the saying that features don't sell but benefits do?

If you cannot help a potential customer understand or realize what he or she will gain by becoming your customer, it will be difficult to win him or her over. Yes, you have the top products manufactured with the best materials or you provide a service that is carried out by the most proficient workers in that state. But who really cares?
You aren't the only one who has top quality products or highly skilled workers.

Examine your business thoroughly to ascertain the top benefits your potential customers will enjoy from your business - and these benefits must be unique.

Don't include a benefit that your competitors already offer, otherwise you'll be judged as an imitator, and you won't be able to achieve your goal (which is snatching your competitors' customers). Think about the benefits you would expect from a business like yours from a customer standpoint.

Continue crafting your USP as you read through these steps.

4. Include an undertaking: By now, you must have included many items in your USP. Prospective customers are supposed to believe you, but why would they trust a new or obscure business?

Some will, but others won't until you give them a guarantee.

That guarantee is the undertaking referenced earlier. Using Domino's Pizza again as an example, in their USP, they promise to deliver your pizza within 30 minutes or let you have it for free if they fail.

An undertaking in your USP also indicates seriousness and credibility. You don't have to explicitly state your undertaking. You can just allude to it. If possible, refer to something that proves that you will actually fulfill your promise.

5. Summarize your USP in one paragraph: Read the benefits, problems, and undertaking you wrote down and summarize them in a short paragraph. This is your first USP draft. Then adjust it to suit your ideal customers (from step 1). Ensure you retain the most salient points during the adjustment.

6. Refine and summarize again: This time, the summary should be a **well-crafted succinct one-sentence USP**. This is the most difficult step of all, and it can be a very involved and wearisome process if this is your first time creating a USP. However, by reading the unique selling propositions of successful businesses, you will get an idea of precisely how your final draft should read and what makes a perfect USP, which will consequently make the process less daunting and easier.

Chapter 5 The Perfect USP

This is one of the shortest chapters in the book but it is this way for a reason. It packs a big punch in a short space. This is how your USP should be too, down to a single hard hitting sentence.

Marketing legend Gary Halbert once said, "You don't have to get it perfect, you just have to get it going."

He also said, "Motion beats Meditation".

Now those truisms aren't always true, but they are most of the time and especially when it comes to marketing. The main point he was trying to get across is that it's more important to take action with something that will work than it is to sit and obsess over making something perfect that you never use because you wasted so much time trying to make it perfect forever.

And speaking of perfect, what makes a perfect USP anyway? Great question!

Features of a Perfect USP

A perfect USP is short, sounds unique, comprehensive, and enticing. It makes potential customers eager to patronize the business in question. Make it emotionally appealing and as short as possible - yes, it can be a phrase if you can summarize it into one. As already stated, leave the features out and focus on the benefits as that is what customers are concerned about.

Do You Have to Create The Perfect USP?

As you might have guessed, the answer is no. An untested USP is not perfect until you have implemented it and tested its effectiveness. Although it's advisable to create several drafts until you create something you can call perfect, you don't have to spend your time perfecting it. Start using your USP first, and then track your progress over time in terms of how many customers you are attracting and how prospective customers are responding to it.

As time goes on, you will gain a clearer understanding of your customers' needs, preferences, and what makes them inclined to purchase from you. When that happens, all you will have to do is tweak your current USP a bit to attract more customers.

Chapter 6 Combining AIDA with PAS For Multiplied Response

Well it's your lucky day. Everything we've covered up to now has been foundational and prepares you extremely well for the selling formulas in this chapter. It's important for you to realize that every piece of content you produce can be equipped with maximum tested and proven selling power embedded in it. It's much like cipher text in an encrypted message in that the person reading it sees one thing, but underneath there is another message. Now this doesn't mean that you are deceiving by any means; it just means there are time-tested and scientifically proven to sell formulas that result in more sales and you can use them in all of your content instead of just the sales page.

Imagine you read two different articles from two different companies in the same industry selling the same product. You read one article that is simply informative and you come away feeling like you may or may not have learned something. You read another informative article, but for some reason, after you finish reading it, you find yourself wanting to find out more information from the company and buy their product.

That is the difference between communicating to simply inform and communicating to inform with proven formulas at work for you. It takes the same space, the same amount of words and can be done in the same time. The difference is, one way results in informing and maybe relationship building with a few sales here and there, but the other way, results in sales multiplied.

Two of the oldest most proven sales formulas are AIDA (Attention Interest Desire Action) and PAS (Problem Agitate Solve). With Get the Click you combine both of these formulas to harness the power of both at the same time and also use tactics like the law of contrast, urgency, scarcity, exclusivity and social proof in a repeatable system for many more sales than any other formulas or tactics alone.

We're going to cover a lot of extremely powerful material in a short space in the next chapter so it will pay to make sure you focus and understand the concepts presented because these tools can help you to make a fortune in business with your marketing.

Chapter 7 The Secret Recipe

We all know at one time, Coca-Cola's secret formula included cocaine as one of its ingredients before pressures resulted in forcing them to remove it. Even without using that drug, their formula for the most part still remained relatively distinct from their competitors. It was reported in recent years by Time magazine and others, that someone had printed the ingredients in an Atlanta newspaper in the late 1970s. It was also reported by insiders that only two people know the entire formula. These two people fly on separate airplanes just in case the airplane crashes and the recipe is safeguarded in a bank vault. That's how valuable and serious they are about keeping the formula and ingredients to themselves.

The thing about recipes and formulas though are just one small change in the amounts of just one of the ingredients can alter the end results to where the final product is nearly unrecognizable and much different from the original. The same is true with direct response formulas. It's not enough to simply know the ingredients to the formula, but it's equally important to know the right order of each component. Each element of the formula performs a specific duty and together, in the right order, they result in a sale. Leave one out or put it in a less effective order than the original and you could have a disaster.

On the other hand, if you can figure a way to extract the best elements from two of the best formulas and combine them with other elements into one formula that works even better when tested, you will have improved upon the best. And that's what has been done for you. You can now enjoy using a formula that does everything the others do, but then goes beyond for you to multiply your results. In the next few pages, you will have examples given so that you are sure to "Get it" as easily as possible. You can take these examples and then adapt them to your own specific market, product, service and offers. And remember, because you have already laid the groundwork with the foundational elements of the formula, which are creating your perfect customer avatar and creating your USP, you're now getting into the nitty-gritty that will allow you to create one well-oiled marketing sales machine after another and use it in all your communications where an action from someone will benefit you and your business.

1. First, what you want to do is get the attention of your prospect.

This means you need to develop a "hook" which will be sure to speak to him/her, reel them in and get them reading every word you have to say. What would be most likely to get the attention of your target market if they saw it in a headline, a video title, blog post title, forum thread title, press release title or the title of an article?

Some tips for getting attention with your content

    A. Use specific numbers when you can.

Example: "Do You Make These 7 Mistakes in Getting More Traffic to Your Website?"

    B. Make a promise of a specific benefit:

Example: "Make $1023.95 a Day Without Doing Any Work at All!"

    C. Make your advertising more valuable by implying the benefit of your reader finding out something just for reading it.

Example: "How to Make $1374.28 a Day Without Doing Any Work!"

    D. Use "Power Words".

Example: Amazing!, Breakthrough!, Groundbreaking!, Revolutionary!, Never-Before-Seen!

This gives you some good understanding of how to get attention with your marketing so you get more people clicking through to your website which ultimately means...You (wait for it)...

...get more clicks and get more traffic!

Okay, so now you know how to get attention. Let's move on to the next element of the formula.

2. Second, you want to stimulate the *interest* of your reader.

Okay, so now think to yourself. Say, "How can I really stimulate the interest of my readers in my target market?"

What would get them interested and keep them interested in what I have to say here? That's right. Get them interested in your content and wanting to find out more.

Here are some ways you can stimulate the interest of your reader

A. Reveal fascinating facts in the form of "Did You Know?" questions.

Example: Did You Know out of all the highest paid copywriters who write sales copy online, Doug Barger converts the most unique visitors into sales? Here's his most powerful secret for generating unbeatable control after unbeatable control...

B. Kill the cat. (Build Curiosity)

Okay, cat lovers, you can stop clawing me now. You know how curiosity killed the cat? Well there's more than one way to skin one. Kidding. I actually love animals and would never hurt one. My 2 favorite cats are both girls named Savannah and Roary. Maybe in future updates I will upload pictures of them in this section to help you remember how to create curiosity.
 But seriously, you can generate interest sky high by "holding back" on the secret sauce until they purchase your big mac and build so much curiosity they'll read every word with intense interest.

Example: This one little known (but extremely powerful) secret for building large fortunes in record time will make you laugh with delight once you see how easy it is to make work for you too!

(Kind of makes you want to know what it is doesn't it? See how it gets your readers interested?)

C. Build Anticipation, "But first...

Introduce the idea you're about to deliver some very exciting and valuable information, but first you need to tell them something else before you do.

This gets people reading with more interest because they can hardly wait to see what it is you're about to tell them.

Try it, it works!

Nothing stimulates more interest than when you're anticipating. Ever been watching one of those television shows where just before the big climax, you see...

To Be Continued...

If so, you know exactly what building anticipation and suspense is all about already. You can use these same elements to your advantage when creating your marketing materials to get more qualified traffic and more clicks and sales from these people in the market for what you have to offer.

Okay, we've wrapped up getting attention and building interest. Now it's time to arouse their _desire_!

(Yep. This is when you channel what they already want and dream about straight into the materials you've created for marketing your products and services.)

It's time to awaken that impulse that screams, "I want it, I want it and I've got to get it now!" Master this one and you're writing your own larger than life paychecks. Onward.

3. Arouse Desire

How do you arouse desire and fan the flames of buying passion?

First you need to create your plan to use as the foundation.

This one simple exercise takes probably no more than five minutes, but can create an internal organizational asset for you that you can use to dramatically increase the success of each new product, each new sales message and each new "touch" or marketing contact you have with your niche market for the rest of the life cycle of your business.

First get out some index cards you know you will keep near your work area and be able to access easily. You might choose to put them in a desk drawer or file cabinet nearby your work station or laptop bag if you're always on the go and work remotely and travel frequently.

Sometimes when you use physical materials like index cards or notebook paper, it helps you to realize it's something "tangible" and important for your business than if it is just another "online" document. However, do feel free to use any type of document or file you would like to use to create and store your list, like a Microsoft word document, open office word document or notepad file. It's not as important exactly which file type you use. The important thing is you're always able to easily access it and edit it in the future when you need to use it.

Use this to make yourself a very specific list like the one following:

Ask yourself these three questions:

1. "What keeps the people in my target market awake at night wishing they had?"

_____

2. "If they could have the perfect, dream-like solution which was the answer to their prayers, what would this look like?"

_____

3. "What do people in my market really want?"

_____

(You may want to make a copy of the page your list is on so you can have it handy and keep on file for easy reference later.)

Now I want you to think about it.

What makes you "want" something?

Would you like to know some ways to awaken and activate the buying passion in your readers?

Here are some ways to arouse desire

A. Drink in the Desert Technique

When you're dehydrated and in the desert dying for a drink of water,

it wouldn't take much to get you to "desire" a tall glass of ice cold water would it?

"Nature's champagne" just became more desirable than ever.

How can you get your prospects to experience that type of thirst for your products and services?

    A. First, you need to make them painfully aware of their problem. Remind them of their problem and how it's urgent they solve it.

Bring that pain the unsolved problem is causing them to the front of their mind and make it the focus of their attention.

Make any type of solution at all seem like it's separated by an eternal gulf that can't be crossed. At this point, they will need to see the need for not only solving their problem, but also have an immense desire to solve their problem urgently! See what you've done there?

Now let's go back to the desert.

Whoever brings them that glass of water is going to look like a savior who is offering them an all-expense paid one way ticket out of hell into eternal paradise!

Hey, if Almighty God chose to present salvation to us in that way, we could certainly do a lot worse in choosing a different model to follow.

Okay, now that the path to your eternal abode is no longer in question, let's look at how to amplify the benefits of your product or service to show the contrast between the problem experienced and the solution offered.

You can do this by explaining the benefits of owning your product or obtaining your services in different ways and how each are used most effectively to produce the results they seek.

You can tell a story where someone, even yourself, goes through the same problem your market is experiencing.

You can show empathy by describing the feelings of how painful it is to go through the problem.

You can then begin to ask your prospect to imagine what life would be like without that problem or if that problem was solved.

Then once the difference between having that problem and having that problem solved is made as clearly contrasted as day from night…

You introduce your product or service as the star of the show!

And like a knight in shining armor, your product or service swoops in to swoon and sweep your prospect off their feet with the same solution they imagined and were dreaming about...the one you just described to them with the benefits of your product or service!

Stories aren't the only way this can be done.

You can also list benefits as "bullets" one after the other building desire. The *key* secret to unlocking the powerful results of using this method is by introducing your product or service as the bridge between where their problem has them and where your product or service can take them!

This makes your product or service the obvious choice to solve their problem. Do you see how powerful this is?

It's the marketing equivalent of offering a man dying of thirst a life-saving drink of water in the desert. This also creates fierce loyalty from your clients and customers and bonds them to you.

And that's not such a bad problem to have is it?

You'll just have to offer them more and more products and services to quench their thirst for more solutions from you!

B. Use "Visual Words and Phrases" like

Imagine, Picture, What if You Could, See Yourself, Visualize, Look at,

When you use words and phrases like this, you can invite your prospect on a journey...

...a wonderful adventure of seeing themselves somewhere in the future enjoying

a higher quality of life as the result of purchasing products and services from you.

Once they are imagining this incredible new world, you offer your product and service as the ticket to admission to the world where their deepest desires are fulfilled in reality.

Can you see yourself doing this now? I can! Well done.
You're now able to help more and more people to the lives they've always dreamed of

(and getting paid royally for the pleasure)

due to increased sales and business!

C. Blind Benefits and Curiosity Combo

This works especially well when creating bulleted lists of benefits.

It's combining the curiosity technique we covered earlier with the visualizing technique from above.

You have now basically created the perfect sales scenario where your prospect feels like a blind person being told of the beauties of sight which they could only experience by having their eyes opened or of course, by purchasing your products or services.

Example: Here are some examples:

*Never worry about money again once you have this one 5 word sentence to use in all of your marketing which increases sales by as much as ten times or more instantly!

*You'll wonder how you ever made it before once you discover how enjoyable it is to turn this automatic money faucet on with just a few clicks of your mouse

*Look how easy it is to save 40 hours off your work week and instantly multiply the productivity (and profitability) of every action you do while "at work"

*See yourself on the tropical beaches of paradise, free from telephones ringing and having the time of your life because you put this unique plan to action

Once you get good at these, you can extract the benefits from each and every
feature of your product or service and really amplify the effects and value of the benefits your new clients and customers receive from you.

In fact, this is one of my favorite methods in the entire formula!

It's because in order to improve your life, you have to have a clear picture of the result you desire first.

D. Using Scarcity, Exclusivity, Urgency and Social Proof

"We want what we cannot have." Ever heard that before?
There's a mythological character named "Tantalus".

He had done something evil or somehow otherwise angered the gods and as a result,

Tantalus's punishment for his act, now a proverbial term for temptation without satisfaction, was to stand in a pool of water under fruit hanging on the low hanging branches of a fruit tree. Each time he would reach for a piece of fruit from the tree,
the branch would suddenly withdraw it from his reach.

Each time he reached down to get a drink of water, the water would recede before he had the chance to get a single drop.

Can you see how this works to build desire?

The word "tantalize" today means to tease, but *not* to please just yet.

You can really build the desire for your products or services by presenting an offer which is irresistible in that it is:

*only available to a select few (Exclusivity)

*only available for a limited time
(Urgency)

*only available in limited quantities
(Scarcity)

*one that has produced results for others
(Social Proof)

You can simply provide testimonials as social proof if you're using a sales letter or tell the story of someone who succeeded when using other methods of marketing.

Well, now you can see how to:

1.Command Attention to arrest your prospects in their tracks for being in your market and look at your marketing leading to your offers

2. Pique Interest in your marketing materials or sales letters to stimulate as much interest as possible in what you are saying so the more they are exposed to, the more they sell themselves on what you'll offer

3. Arouse Desire so they are craving your products and services as what they want so they feel they,
"Have to Get This Now!"

So, now it's time to **actually motivate the actions you want your prospect to take so your visitors *click through* to your website**.

This is where your Quality Traffic comes from! This is where you literally "Get the Click".

The reason it's a higher quality than average traffic is because you have used all the *qualifying* elements of this formula to ensure
each visitor:

A. Is painfully aware of their problem and need for your solution

B. Made interested already by your content

C. Qualified to benefit from your offer because they desire it

So now it's time to motivate them to take...

4. Action

There's no way around it, you need to be:

1. Clear

2. Specific

3. Direct

with your "Call to Action".

Your "call to action" is where you tell your reader or prospect exactly what you want them to do.

It's amazing how many people get this part wrong before they learn. When it comes time to tell your prospect what to do, it's no time to be vague or dilly dally around.

But make your call to action tight, clear, specific and assume you will get the click.

Here are some good examples that have worked for me and my clients:

    A. "To Discover How to (Benefit Here) ,
Just click here now--> (your website link here)

    B. "Sick of Struggling with (problem here)?
Click here to finally get (solution here)   (website link here)

Those are 2 basic "templates" you can model for your own call to actions. This will save you a lot of time when creating your content, because now you have a proven system to use which you can just plug in your specific custom details and be ready to go with it.

Now, as you know, like all formulas and secrets, this only works for you when you use it!
So, use it at every opportunity to experience more profits, sales and revenue from all your marketing and business for life!

About The Author

Born and raised in a small suburb about twenty miles outside Nashville, Tennessee, for a long time I worked in sales and eventually was promoted to management and became a corporate sales trainer. In 2006, due to the opportunity I saw to live my entrepreneurship vision, after experiencing some encouraging initial successes marketing business opportunities online part time, I quit my fulltime job and went into internet marketing fulltime.

Since then, I have written and published several e-books, websites, courses and training as well as obtained my certification as a business success coach. Having mastered direct response copywriting after writing dozens of sales letters, landing pages, email campaigns and other marketing and advertising campaigns and learning from each one, I began a thriving copywriting business with loyal clients ranging from the information marketer running their business solo to multinational corporations with multi-millions of dollars in annual revenues, creating unrivaled conversion response rates and helping businesses grow more sales, profits, revenues, new customers and new income streams than they first believed possible .

It's truly been an exciting adventure and although not always glamorous. The lessons learned the hard way through trial and error usually involved plenty of short term failures leading to breakthrough success sometimes just before I'd be tempted to give up the pursuit of my ambitions.

It's now my passion as an author and coach to help equip others to live and achieve their goals as entrepreneurs without having to learn it all the hard way or on your own. And help you get from where you are now to where you want to be.

I enjoy connecting with you here and eagerly look forward to working with you for years as we work to achieve all your goals of financial independence and success as entrepreneurs. As your coach, I am fully vested in holding you accountable to reach your goals and expect you to put the effort required to create a lifestyle of true financial independence and success, even when the going gets tough and you're tempted to quit, like all of us have been tempted to do from time to time.

Remember, it's the steady plodding that leads to wealth and if you keep moving toward the direction of your goals with focus and consistency, there is no limit to what you can achieve financially. You really can do this if you will commit to doing it!

Questions or comments? E-mail me at NextLevel@EntrepreneurshipSuccessSecrets.com or find me on the following social networks:

Facebook: http://facebook.com/DougBarger
Twitter: http://twitter.com/DougBarger
LinkedIn: http://www.linkedin.com/in/dougbarger

More from Doug Barger

If you would like to get on the fast track to lasting success with your own entrepreneurship endeavors,   you should definitely check out Entrepreneurship Success Secrets "Discover the Entrepreneur Within You!" It features proven strategies, tips, mindset and marketing help as well as plenty of great ways for you to start your own business and income streams. It's available on the Kindle Store now and you can also get it in paperback.

Visit: http://amazon.com/author/dougbarger for more details and to buy other books published by Doug Barger.

One Last Thing...

When you turn the page, Kindle will give you the opportunity to rate this book and share your thoughts on Facebook and Twitter. If you believe the book is worth sharing, please would you take a few seconds to let your friends know about it on all your social networks? If it turns out to make a difference in their lives, they'll be forever grateful to you and so will I. (Thank you!) ☺

All the best,

Doug

www.ingramcontent.com/pod-product-compliance
Lightning Source LLC
Chambersburg PA
CBHW051302170526
45165CB00004B/1814